T0145023

AN UNEXPECTED FRIENDSHIP

K. K. Hodge

WestBow Press books may be ordered through booksellers or by contacting:

WestBow Press
A Division of Thomas Nelson & Zondervan
1663 Liberty Drive
Bloomington, IN 47403
www.westbowpress.com
844-714-3454

ISBN: 978-1-6642-9178-2 (sc)
ISBN: 978-1-6642-9179-9 (e)

Library of Congress Control Number: 2023902290

Print information available on the last page.

WestBow Press rev. date: 02/13/2023

WESTBOW
P R E S S®
A DIVISION OF THOMAS NELSON
& ZONDERVAN

AN UNEXPECTED FRIENDSHIP

One chilly morning in March,
we ventured out to an exotic animal sale.
There were a variety of critters,
some furry, some feathered, both male & female.

Before the day came to an end,
we made a quite unique purchase.
We quickly fell in love,
and nothing or no one could deter us.

A soft as fleece, baby kangaroo
became our newest furry family member.
He fit in so perfectly,
with his beautiful features and grand splendor.

We bottle fed and diapered him,
and he hopped around our homestead.
He laid around and watched TV,
and he even slept in the middle of our bed!

A few months passed by
with a little kangaroo living in our home.
Who would have thought
our next family member would be an Axis fawn?

We never could have dreamed
that this quite unusual animal pair
would develop a friendship,
an unexpected kinship indeed very rare.

For several weeks we lived
with a deer and a Roo inside.
We became quite attached,
our love for them we couldn't hide.

We knew they would someday
have to move out to the barnyard,
but deciding when to move them
turned out to be very hard!

Roo's legs grew longer,
and as he stretched out those legs,
he started kicking us out
of our very own king-size bed!

We knew the time had come
to move them both out to the barn.
My head knew the facts,
but my heart was just torn.

How would my two furry babies
make it out in the great outdoors?
They were raised in our home
with windows, walls, and doors.

This human mama worried
that they would feel lost and all alone,
Their people and one another
is all they have ever known.

The worry was in vain.
I had nothing at all to fear.
An amazing lesson was learned
from my Roo and my deer.

Two very different species,
unrelated, very different, and not kin,
turned out to be the wonderful,
truly unexpected very best of friends.

Roo and Bucky show us how to love
others even when they're different from us.
A furry, long tailed, hopping kangaroo
and a long-legged, running deer didn't fuss.

They overlooked one another's differences
and developed an unconditional love.
They loved each other as instructed
from our Father in heaven above.

Jesus says the first commandment
is to love God above all others,
but the second commandment reminds us
to love our sisters and our brothers.

We are to love our neighbors,
and that means everyone we meet.
We must love all people.
This command bears a repeat.

19

It's easy to love some people like
Our friends who are like us,
but we can't just love the easy ones.
God doesn't want us to show bias.

Skin color may vary in shade and tone,
and our neighbor may not talk or walk as we do.
They may even be confined to a chair
with wheels and perhaps it may have a motor too.

They may wear glasses or have freckles
that cover their little noses.
They may like blue violet flowers,
instead of pretty red roses.

Yes, our neighbors and friends
may come in a variety of sizes and shapes.
God made each one unique,
but He did not make any mistakes.

If we take time to pray
and study God's Word,
we can love like Jesus,
and share what we've heard.

Give it a try, make a new friend.
Love like Jesus loves, on Him you can depend.
Soon you too may find that you have
a truly unexpected very best friend!

"Teacher, which is the great commandment in the Law?" And he said to him, "You shall love the Lord your God with all your heart and all your soul and with all your mind. This is the great and first commandment. And a second is like it: You shall love your neighbor as yourself. On these two commandments depend all the Law and the Prophets."

—Matthew 22:36-40 ESV

Printed in the United States
by Baker & Taylor Publisher Services